101 Ways
to
Get More Customers
Online and Offline
for Under $100

Disclaimer:

Although the author and publisher have made every effort to ensure that the information in this book was correct at press time, the author and publisher do not assume and hereby disclaim any liability to any party for any loss, damage, or disruption caused by errors or omissions, whether such errors or omissions result from negligence, accident, or any other cause. No part of this book may be reproduced or transferred in any form or by any means, graphic, electronic, or mechanical, including photocopying, recording, taping, or by any information storage retrieval system, without the written permission of the author.

The accuracy and completeness of information provided herein and opinions stated herein are not guaranteed or warranted to produce any particular results, and the advice and strategies, contained herein may not be suitable for every individual or business. The author and Coach Me (vic) Pty Ltd shall not be liable for any loss incurred as a consequence of the use and application, directly or indirectly, of any information presented in this work. This publication is designed to provide opinion in regard to the subject matter covered. The author has used his efforts in preparing this book. Sold with the understanding, the author is not engaged in rendering legal, accounting, or other professional services. If legal advice or expert assistance is required, the services of a competent professional should be sought.

About the Author:

Known internationally as *The Sales King*, Aaron Sansoni is one of Australia's Leading Sales Experts.

He has a long trail of success stories in 4 continents and has been at the Sales and Marketing Coaching and Consulting forefront for over a decade.

Aaron has trained and coached thousands of business owners and sales professionals from across many industries, helping them break through and achieve phenomenal results.

His training has generated tens of millions of dollars for the people and companies he has coached.

Aaron is the Founder and CEO of Coach Me, a leading specialist SME business coaching firm, as well as a sought-after Key Note Speaker having shared the stage with the likes of Sir Richard Branson and other business leaders across Australia, Asia, USA and the UK.

Introduction

'**The Sales King**' is an International Sales Training Company founded from years of business, sales and marketing experience in 4 continents.

As the creator of The Sales King, I'm incredibly proud of the success of the 1000's of clients worldwide who have attended an event, completed our programs or have been coached and achieved their dreams.

From Australia to Singapore, America, the UK, China and countless other countries, The Sales King is a universal sales system for the 21st Century.

This book was created as an easy-to-use and useful guide for small businesses to increase their sales at a small cost utilising both online and offline ideas.

I invite you to share your favourite ideas and success stories using these ideas with The Sales King community on our Facebook fan page:

www.facebook.com/thesalesking

or on twitter using the hash tag: #thesalesking or drop me an email to:

enquires@aaronsansoni.com

I look forward to hearing from you, and ENJOY! All the best

Aaron Sansoni
Author- Business Coach- Sales Trainer-Entrepreneur

Share your favourite idea or success story
with other readers
On Twitter using the hash tag: **#thesalesking**
Or on the Official Facebook fanpage:
www.facebook.com/thesalesking

One contributor will be selected
to receive a free copy of
**The Sales King – Ultimate System
by Aaron Sansoni worth $4997**

Dedication

This book is dedicated to all the hardworking small business owners around the world.

Keep the passion, keep the focus and achieve your dreams.

All the Best

Aaron

Table of contents

Online Ideas

Online Ideas

www.aaronsansoni.com

IDEA 1: Create a free Website

Cost: Zero

Why do it:

If you don't have a website already... get with the 21st Century! More and more people are going online to look for information, catalogues, businesses, and everything in between. Every business, no matter what it is, should have a Website. Starting with a free Website is a great idea and most if not all the free Websites have Website builders to help you create one without you needing to have any previous web design experience at all.

How to do it:

1. You can either do a search on one of the search engines (Google, Yahoo, Bing, Ask, etc.) for free Website builders, or you can use the ones listed in the resources below.

2. Find a template on the free Website builder. Make sure the template will work for what you want on your Website and

then plan your Website.

3. If your business is an online one, you may want to optimise it for search engines to easily find, which means more visitors to your Website. Refer to Idea #3 for more information about keywords.

4. Either write the content yourself, or get someone to do it for you if you're not a great writer. Remember that your Website is like a showcase for your business it's the first impression your potential clients get of your business, so make it a good one.

Resource/s:

Free Website builders:

www.weebly.com

www.wix.com

www.vistaprint.com

Online freelance content writers:

www.elance.com

www.freelancewriting.com

IDEA 2: Include your Website on respectable directories

Cost: Free for www.dmoz.org; $69.95 annually for www.goguides.org.

Why do it:
There are numerous reasons for listing your Website on respectable directories. Firstly, consumers check online directories in much the same way as they would have referred to a telephone directory in the past. Secondly, people who search on online directories are looking for something specific, so they are "qualified" traffic – meaning, they are more likely to do business with you if they find you. Also, search engines rank your Website based on the incoming links to it from respectable sites, so your page ranking is likely to go up over time too.

How to do it:
1. Dmoz is a good directory and it's free! It can be very difficult to get listed, but once you are in, your rankings will improve

dramatically. Keep submitting monthly until they accept.

2. Sign up to get listed at GoGuides.

Resource/s:

Respectable, affordable web directories:

www.dmoz.org

www.goguides.org

Share your favourite idea or success story
with other readers
On Twitter using the hash tag: **#thesalesking**
Or on the Official Facebook fanpage:
www.facebook.com/thesalesking

One contributor will be selected
to receive a free copy of
**The Sales King – Ultimate System
by Aaron Sansoni worth $4997**

IDEA 3: Focus on Keywords

Cost: Zero if you do it yourself. $25-50 if you use a person to write you a report.

Why do it:
Keywords are the words people use to search for products or information on the Internet, using search engines like Google. Keywords in the online world are absolutely vital. Without focused keywords, your Website is unlikely to be found by potential customers. The Websites that search engines put on the first page when someone enters a keyword search are those that get the most traffic, and also the ones who have focused on keywords in their Website. This is organic traffic not paid placement. A website without focused keywords is a billboard in the desert.

How to do it:
1. Jot down the words your clients would use to most aptly describe your business.
2. Do keyword research with a free keyword

tool. The best keywords or phrases to use are those with a lot of searches every month, but with a low amount of competition. Use the best words or phrases on your Website.

3. Research focused keywords and how best to use them on your Website.

4. Post a job on Elance for someone to do this for you for around $25 - $50. Simple.

Resource/s:

Keyword Research:

www.googlekeywordtool.com

www.elance.com

IDEA 4: Google AdWords

Cost: There's no minimum spend requirement – the amount you pay for AdWords is up to you. You can, for instance, set a daily budget of five dollars and a maximum cost of ten cents for each click on your ad.

Why do it:
Google Adwords are those small "boxes" of ads that are put on the results page of a search. The reason they are such a good idea, is because many times people are not even aware that they are ads, or even if they are, people are likely to click on them first because the ads appear before the rest of the results on a search page. They are not expensive, and it's a really quick way of driving traffic to your Website fast. And most importantly you're charged only if someone clicks your ad, not when your ad is displayed. Don't forget, Google is the biggest search engine on the planet... enough said.

How to do it:

1. Put simply, you pay Google to run text ads for you based on your keywords. In other words, if your business is about weight loss, and one of your keywords is "weight loss", Google will run your ad on the search page results when someone searches on "weight loss".

2. Learn more about Google AdWords, and create an account with them. It's a good way to get visitors to your Website fast.

3. Put a limit on how much you're prepared to spend, and Google will stop running your ad when the money runs out.

Resource/s:

Google AdWords:

www.google.com/ads/adwords

IDEA 5: Advertise on Facebook

Cost: There's no set cost for adverts or Sponsored Stories and as an advertiser, you can control how much you spend for each campaign by setting a daily or lifetime budget. So you can get some traction for under $100 with a well thought out plan.

Why do it:
With such a large, global, usage base of over one billion and the ability to really target users that suit your business, Facebook advertising is a no brainer for your business.

How to do it:
1. Build your Facebook Page if you don't already have one – super easy and quick (and Free). Check out www.facebook.com/thesalesking to see The Sales King fan page as an example.
2. Connect with people. Get people to like your Page. Create several adverts target-based on location, demographics and in-

terests.

3. Engage with quality content. Post quality updates and promote your posts with adverts to engage your customers and their friends.

4. Influence the friends of your fans.

Resource/s:

Keyword Research:

www.facebook.com/advertising

Share your favourite idea or success story
with other readers
On Twitter using the hash tag: **#thesalesking**
Or on the Official Facebook fanpage:
www.facebook.com/thesalesking

One contributor will be selected
to receive a free copy of
**The Sales King – Ultimate System
by Aaron Sansoni worth $4997**

IDEA 6: Showcase and sell your goods for free on top e-commerce companies

Cost: Zero.

Why do it:

We all buy from places like eBay. Any traffic that comes to e-commerce websites is traffic that is "qualified" – these people are looking for things to buy. They have done their research, and now they are looking to buy goods. If your products are on display, they are more likely to be viewed, and purchased.

How to do it:

1. Research e-commerce companies to list your products for free, or use the resources below as a start.
2. Make sure you select the right e-commerce company for your target market. For example, Etsy only promotes certain goods, such as handmade or vintage

products or craft supplies, and attracts
potential customers looking for these particular goods.

3. Some e-commerce companies also list
   services, so if your business provides a
   service, you are not excluded from this
   idea, just look for the right e-commerce
   company.

4. Simply start a free account with the right
   e-commerce site to start showcasing and
   promoting your products.

Resource/s:

E-commerce sites:

www.etsy.com

www.ebay.com

IDEA 7: Use a domain name which features your main keyword

Cost: It will cost you roughly $11 annually to register a domain name.

Why do it:
If you're a small to medium size business, your brand will not be as well known as a large company's brand. They can get away with putting their company name as their domain name. In fact, that's how Websites began – by using their company name. But today, if you want to be found more easily when people search for what you sell, using a domain name that contains your main keyword is vital. For instance, if McDonalds were not as well known as they are, www.mcdonalds.com would not be as effectively found as "www.burgers.com", because people are not looking for "McDonalds", they are looking for "burgers".

How to do it:

1. Firstly, do keyword research with Google's Keyword Tool to determine your main keywords – the words you want to be known for online. The best keywords to choose are those with high monthly searches and low competition. Select the best one for your business (use the information in idea #3 to find the right keywords for you).

2. Then check if the domain name is available – you can use Namecheap to do this for free.

Resource/s:

Keyword Research:
www.googlekeywordtool.com

Domain name availability:
www.namecheap.com

IDEA 8: Traffic exchange sites

Cost: Zero, unless you upgrade.

Why do it:
The objective of using a traffic exchange site is two-fold: to get more potential customers viewing your Website, and to improve your search engine page rank because you have more incoming links to your Website. By improving your search engine page rank you go up the organic Google rankings!

How to do it:
1. Quite simply, the aim of a traffic exchange site is for other people to view your ads (which you create for free on their site), and for you to view the ads of other Websites. The more you view, the more credits you earn for others to view your Website.

2. Simply go to the resource below and sign up for a free account. Most traffic exchange sites will provide step by step

instructions as to what you should do.

Resource/s:

Traffic exchange:

www.trafficswarm.com

Share your favourite idea or success story
with other readers
On Twitter using the hash tag: **#thesalesking**
Or on the Official Facebook fanpage:
www.facebook.com/thesalesking

One contributor will be selected
to receive a free copy of
**The Sales King – Ultimate System
by Aaron Sansoni worth $4997**

IDEA 9: Social Media

Cost: Zero.

Why do it:

As people spend most of their online time using Social Media sites, they are one of the easiest ways to get traffic to your Website fast. More and more people are becoming social media savvy, and if you want to stay up to date with trends, you need to know what's being talked about. While you should do your own independent research to see what's out there – to begin with stick with the biggest sites as shown below.

How to do it:

1. There are 100's of social media sites. Before you start wading through them all, be sure about what you aim to achieve from each one. Research each one from a business perspective first, and then create a social media strategy to keep it focused. The objective is to get people to share

your content and participate in your business and on your Website.

2. You should always encourage people to interact with you through social media.

3. We suggest you choose 2 – 4 social media sites to be active on, and consider using a free resource website to update all your social networks at once.

Resource/s:

The most popular social media sites:
Twitter, Facebook, LinkedIn, StumbleUpon, Digg, Delicious, Pinit, Reddit, Flickr, Foursquare, Google +.

Update all social networks at once:
https://seesmic.com

IDEA 10: Text link ads

Cost: Approximately $99.

Why do it:
The objective with text link ads is to drive more traffic to your Website and improve your search engine page ranking as a result of the incoming links going to your site. While text link ads are a good idea, they shouldn't be your first to tryout; get the keywords and social media going first.

How to do it:
1. Research "text link ads" Websites, or start with the ones below.
2. Simply choose a plan and open an account.
3. Take into consideration that you may only really start to see the benefits in 3 – 6 months time.

Resource/s:
 Text link ads companies:
  www.textlinkads.com
  www.textlinkbrokers.com

IDEA 11: Have an online contest

Cost: You can do it for under $100; the cost will depend on the prizes you give away.

Why do it:
Where there are things of value to be given away, there will be people. If you do it well, you will increase the amount of traffic on your Website by having an online contest, and create a stir as well. People see the benefit of joining contests, because they may come away with something of value. It's a great way of getting attention. But don't launch it until you have some site traffic!

How to do it:
1. You can have all sorts of contests that you combine with your social networks as well as your Website.
2. Get creative; do something fun that people can get excited about. Offer prizes of value to people who may be interested in

35

your products to encourage them to enter.

3. Create a lot of awareness about the contest in as many ways as possible.

4. Develop a strategy and a plan before you take any action. List your objectives, timeframe, theme, find sponsors, etc.

5. Think about what you will do – some ideas: scavenger hunt where visitors need to find something on your Website, or they have to submit a poem or story or complete a survey.

Resource/s:
Instantly Increase Your Sales in a Downward Economy – Section on "Irresistible Offers"

www.aaronsansoni.com

IDEA 12: Blogging

Cost: $5 a month for hosting plus approximately $10 for a domain name.

Why do it:
Blogging is the 4th biggest online activity. People enjoy blogs because they are written informally and a lot of information can be gathered from them. Blog sites attract more Website traffic because of all the content that is usually contained in them. The objective of a blog is to provide valuable content, and to get as many people as possible to enter your Website and read your posts, and make comments.

How to do it:
1. Once you have a blog, you can comment on other people's blogs, leaving your link there for others to find you, driving more traffic to your site (see idea #14).
2. If you don't already have a blog, select a domain name based on keyword research (refer to idea #3 – keyword research and

37

idea #7 – domain names above)

3. Select a Website host (see resources) and create an account for your Wordpress or Blogger site to be hosted on.

4. Customise the template you choose and start posting as much as possible, remembering to use targeted keywords (refer to idea #3).

Resource/s:

Hosts:

www.bluehost.com
www.godaddy.com
www.hostgator.com

IDEA 13: Comment on other blogs

Cost: Zero.

Why do it:

By commenting on other blogs, you are creating "brand awareness" and online presence with your comment, with the aim of driving as much traffic back to your site as possible. People will click back to your site if what you say is of value to them. If you comment on quality blogs, and people link to your Website from that blog, it helps develop the credibility of your Website with search engines, which in turn leads to a higher search engine page ranking.

How to do it:

1. Find blogs that are in your niche and list them to your "blog database" for easy access.

2. Once you've commented on a few blogs, you will start noticing those who allow you to comment with a link back to your

site, or those who allow you to post with your Facebook account etc. The point is that there are some blogs which won't benefit you to make comments on, because they don't have the capability for you to leave your mark so that their other visitors can link back to your Website if they think what you say is interesting.

3. Make sure your comments are of value – remember that you are creating "brand awareness" with your comment, with the aim of driving as much traffic back to your site as possible. People will only click back to your site if what you say is of value to them.

Resource/s: None.

IDEA 14: Answer people's questions in Q & A forums

Cost: Zero

Why do it:

Just like commenting on other blogs, by answering questions well, you are creating "brand awareness" and an online presence of your expertise. People will click back to your site if what you say is valuable. If you comment on quality Q&A forums and people link to your Website from that forum, it helps develop the credibility of your Website with search engines, which in turn leads to a higher search engine page ranking.

How to do it:

1. Do a search for Question and Answer forums.
2. Make sure the forums address your target market, and provide questions you can effectively answer. Also ensure that it benefits you to spend time on that forum by

41

adding a link back to your Website.

3. If you want to get traffic from this method, take the time to answer well.

4. If necessary, find forums that are located in your area.

Resource/s:

Q&A Forum:

www.answers.yahoo.com

http://uk.answers.yahoo.com

www.question.com

Share your favourite idea or success story
with other readers
On Twitter using the hash tag: **#thesalesking**
Or on the Official Facebook fanpage:
www.facebook.com/thesalesking

One contributor will be selected
to receive a free copy of
The Sales King – Ultimate System
by Aaron Sansoni worth $4997

IDEA 15: Submit your Website to major search engines

Cost: Zero for basic package.

Why do it:

The reason you should submit your Website to major search engines is because they often take time to "crawl" to new Websites (if yours is new), or to register updates from your Website. By submitting your site to them instead of waiting for them to "crawl" you will speed the process up. This of course favourably impacts the amount of visitors to your Website.

How to do it:

1. Many times Website hosts have partnered with SEO (Search Engine Optimisation) companies to provide you with free ways of submitting your Website to the major search engines, but you can find your own if you want to, or you can do it yourself directly with the major search engines, such as Google, Yahoo, Bing.

Resource/s:

SEO company to help you submit your site to search engines – free for basic package:

www.attracta.com

www.elance.com (post an SEO job and choose the most suitable applicant)

Share your favourite idea or success story
with other readers
On Twitter using the hash tag: **#thesalesking**
Or on the Official Facebook fanpage:
www.facebook.com/thesalesking

One contributor will be selected
to receive a free copy of
The Sales King – Ultimate System
by Aaron Sansoni worth $4997

IDEA 16: Target your content to those who are most likely to share it

Cost: Zero if you do it yourself or around $30 if you have it written for you.

Why do it:

If you can address your content towards these people (if they are your target audience), you will strike gold as far as sharing is concerned. The "gold" is that more people will come to your Website and share it, and in turn, you will make more sales. The more people know about what you do, the better your sales prospects.

How to do it:

1. Some readers are more inclined to share than others. The first "qualifying" factor is that the reader has to be interested in the topic you've posted. Then you have to grip them with interesting, valuable information.

2. The readers more likely to share your content via social media are those who have social media accounts of their own. Make sure you have social media 'share' buttons on your site and relevant pages.

3. The readers most likely to share are those who have their own blogs and attach importance on social media. Given how tech and social media savvy many of us are these days, these readers can include anyone from the 'mummy' bloggers, to students and business people. The important thing is that you select within your target audience, or someone that has influence over your target audience. Here is a big tip; make sure you have loads of your keywords in the content on your site, this will help your SEO.

4. You may want to try asking your readers to share your content!

Resource/s:

www.elance.com – get articles or content written for you, just post a job advert.

IDEA 17: Guest blog

Cost: Zero.

Why do it:

Blogs with a high amount of traffic and interaction can do wonders for your own Website. If you write for a blog like this, it can drive a lot of traffic to your site, as their visitors click on the link back to you, and because of the page ranking of this high traffic blog, it tells search engines that the link is from a quality site, which increases their trust in your site, and which will in turn raise your page ranking and therefore increase traffic to your site.

How to do it:

1. You can either do a search on "submit a guest post", or "become guest writer", or something to that effect. Go to about page 5 of the search results – these sites will accept more readily than the ones on the first page results, who already probably get many offers.

2. Keep in mind, however, that you want to guest write on sites that have a good page ranking.

3. Or start by going to the resource below and registering to be a guest writer.

Resource/s:

Guest writing site to get you started:

www.guestblogit.com

Share your favourite idea or success story
with other readers
On Twitter using the hash tag: **#thesalesking**
Or on the Official Facebook fanpage:
www.facebook.com/thesalesking

One contributor will be selected
to receive a free copy of
The Sales King – Ultimate System
by Aaron Sansoni worth $4997

IDEA 18: Use online tools to help you increase Website traffic

Cost: Zero.

Why do it:

If you don't analyse what works and what doesn't, you won't know what to continue with in your marketing efforts, and what to stop doing. When coaching clients I call this 'Testing and Measuring'. You can only make improvements if you know what's going on, and why. This is where Analytics come in. Getting organised online is important because you can really get lost in cyberspace with everything that's available and lose focus. And you can waste a lot of time! Using a keyword tool is important because keywords drive traffic to your site.

How to do it:

1. Make use of Google Reader – get organised by letting Google Reader keep track

of things you want to read on the Internet. It's like creating your own personalised magazine. Keep yourself updated on the things you need to know to increase your web traffic.

2. Use Google Analytics – measure your Website's statistics and see what works and what doesn't.

3. Keep Google Keyword Toolbox close! It's a vital tool for keyword research. Using the right keywords and having a keyword strategy in place for your site will definitely bring you more customers.

Resource/s:

Online Tools:

www.googlekeywordtool.com

www.google.com/reader

www.google.com/analytics

IDEA 19: Bring value to a hot online discussion

Cost: Zero.

Why do it:

The reason for finding hot discussions is that you know there will be lots of people reading and commenting on it, and if they see your input, and if it's of value, they will link back to your site to find out more about you.

How to do it:

1. Find discussions on the Web that are hot topics – you can find these at the resources below.
2. This will drive more, good quality traffic to your site.

Resource/s:

Hot News Sites:

www.topsy.com

www.wesmirch.com

www.popURLs.com

IDEA 20: Create a "Best Of" list on your Website

Cost: Zero.

Why do it:
Your chosen "best of" Websites are likely to link back to your site because you are promoting them. When they do that, it creates quality links back to your site, which is good for search engine rankings, and will increase your traffic.

How to do it:
1. Think of what types of "best of" lists you could make for your niche. Examples could be "best weight loss Websites", "best gifts Websites", etc. Or you could have a "we recommend" list, and ask your visitors to also recommend sites.
2. Make sure you have something to define what makes them the "best of"; don't just list any sites randomly.
3. Notify your chosen "best of" Websites, who are likely to link back to your site

because you are promoting them, and they will want others to know. Adding them to "best of" lists or recommended sites will lead to joint ventures, as people feel a need to reciprocate.

Resource/s:

Ideas:

www.listsofbests.com

IDEA 21: Use Google Keyword Tool when writing your web content

Cost: Zero if you do it yourself, or $25 -$100 for someone to add your keywords to your site.

Why do it:

If you want people to be able to find you easily on the Internet, then you need to write your web content in a way that gets you found by search engines. For every blog or article that you up-load onto your site, they should contain your main keywords.

How to do it:

1. First refer to idea #3 for keyword help.
2. Use the Google Keyword Tool for the best keywords to use when writing your web content.
3. Keep in mind that the best words to use are of course those related to your niche, and those who have high monthly search

rates coupled with low competition.

4. Or post a job on Elance for someone to do this for you for around $25 - $100

Resource/s:

www.googlekeywordtool.com
www.elance.com

Share your favourite idea or success story
with other readers
On Twitter using the hash tag: **#thesalesking**
Or on the Official Facebook fanpage:
www.facebook.com/thesalesking

One contributor will be selected
to receive a free copy of
The Sales King – Ultimate System
by Aaron Sansoni worth $4997

IDEA 22: Giveaways for list subscribers

Cost: $19 a month for an auto responder service.

Why do it:
You give something free and of value to visitors if they subscribe with you, it's great for them and it also induces the law of reciprocity. Then you keep them on a list to send info to regularly so as to keep in touch with them, so that once you have gained their trust, you have more chance of selling your products/services to them. This has been shown to be one of the most effective ways of getting sales online, but it has to be done properly and it takes time and nurture to create responsive databases.

How to do it:
1. Think of things you could give away online such as a checklist, task list, video, webinar etc.
2. Once you've decided, create it and make it something of value in your niche.

3. In exchange for the giveaway, people need to complete an "opt-in" form on your site, which consists of inserting their name and email address for instance, which lists them as a subscriber.

4. You need to do this with an auto re-sponder service, which provides the tools to create the opt-in form, and keeps a list of your subscribers who you can keep in touch with via email.

Resource/s:

Auto responders:

www.mailchimp.com

www.aweber.com

www.getresponse.com

IDEA 23: Email campaigns

Cost: $19 a month for an auto responder service.

Why do it:
Email campaigns create hype and will give you attention and create sales if done properly. You will need to have a list of people already in order to have an email campaign. Using the last idea will help when you are ready for this campaign strategy.

How to do it:
1. A campaign is using a set of emails on a subscriber in order to get them to do something you want them to do. In other words, if you're launching a new product, you would send a "pre-launch" email, then a launch email, then another just before you launch, and then one after you launch.
2. It's a good idea to get a copywriter to write these, but if you can't afford one, try to emulate others who have had success

with their campaigns. The most important aspect is to get your subscribers to actually open your email, so your subject header is of utmost importance.

3. An auto responder service will manage everything for you; you just need to get creative with your content.

Resource/s:

Auto responders:

www.mailchimp.com

www.aweber.com

www.getresponse.com

IDEA 24: Viral marketing

Cost:
Depends on what you do. The more creative you are the more impact you can have at a lower cost, however if you need a higher budget consider approaching another small business and creating a viral marketing campaign together (ensuring of course they have your same target market but are not a direct competitor). I've created one with a client that cost $600 and returned $200,000...

Why do it:
The objective of viral marketing is to spread something to as many people as possible, by making it so interesting, whacky or unique that people just "have to" share it with friends, who in turn "have to" share it with their friends and family and so it goes on.

Example: The Australian Government promoted what they described simply as "the best job in the world" with a massively successful Internet campaign. The job paid $100,000 for a 6-month contract to be caretaker of a series of islands in the Great Barrier Reef (off Australia's coast). The point of this position was to have the person selected for the job broadcast weekly video blogs promoting the area. The website for the contest received a million hits the day after its launch and the campaign attracted over 34,000 applicants and generated over $70 million worth of global publicity. The publicity continued even after applications closed as the winner had to do regular video posts, blogs and promote the islands over an array of social networks.

How to do it:

1. Think of a way to use the principle of viral marketing that would be right for your niche, and right for your business. It's not easy, but if you can get it right, you will create a really positive viral marketing campaign!

2. Research other viral marketing examples for ideas. Check YouTube for videos that people love and see how you can tweak and copy the idea for your business.

Resource/s:

Example of the above Viral Marketing Campaign:

http://youtube/5Smi3TuY5Lg

IDEA 25: Videos and video blogging

Cost:
Zero if you already have the equipment. If not you can get a second hand camera that can record video on eBay for under $100.

Why do it:
Videos are big. People enjoy them more than reading, possibly because they don't have to read the information, and what may take 10 minutes to read can be conveyed in one minute by video, so it saves people time. It's also often more entertaining than reading an article – especially for visual people like me!

How to do it:
1. What you need: camera, mobile phone or webcam to make a video, firewire, usb or usb2 to connect the camera to the computer and editing software.
2. Create a YouTube account and add your videos.

3. Upload the video to your Website by simply adding the YouTube or Viddler URL.

4. All video descriptions should point back to your site so that when they are embedded you still get organic traffic.

Resource/s:

Browse or upload videos:

www.youtube.com

Online video features:

www.viddler.com

IDEA 26: Join online forums in your niche

Cost: Zero.

Why do it?

Emotion trumps all. No matter what your business is about, it's about people, and people are driven by emotions. Forums are generally for people who share the same emotion about something. If you contribute on a forum, and contribute in a meaningful way, you're connecting with the audience on the same 'part of the map' that they are currently on, hopefully resulting in traffic and customers to your Website.

How to do it:

1. Do a simple online search for forums in your niche.

2. Before you go ahead and sign up, make sure there's a way you can point back to your Website. Oftentimes forums won't have the capabilities of allowing their

members to have a way of pointing back, so make sure of this.

3. Forums have policies that you need to follow, or you will be kicked off.

4. Never provide feedback that simply looks like a cheap advertisement, but always provide value. Remember your brand is one of the most important things in business.

Resource/s: None.

IDEA 27: Coupon codes

Cost: Zero.

Why do it:
Coupon codes encourage people to buy your goods, because people love getting things for less. You can create coupon codes that expire on a certain day (very handy if you're using them in an email campaign) and you can give a coupon code that expires the next day. This creates a sense of urgency and people are more likely to make a decision on the spot than to "think on it".

How to do it:
1. If you have coupon code software, you can give your potential buyers a code they need to enter when purchasing a product from you.
2. Or go to the resource below and download the free coupon code software.
3. Or get your web designer to create it.

Resource/s:

Free coupon code software:
www.imsoftxtreme.com/coupon-codes

Share your favourite idea or success story
with other readers
On Twitter using the hash tag: **#thesalesking**
Or on the Official Facebook fanpage:
www.facebook.com/thesalesking

One contributor will be selected
to receive a free copy of
The Sales King – Ultimate System
by Aaron Sansoni worth $4997

IDEA 28: Register at Google Places, Yahoo Local and Bing if you're a local biz

Cost: Zero.

Why do it:

Consumers check on these local directories in much the same way as they would a telephone directory. Because they are searching locally, it tells you they may already be close to buying something specific, which makes them "qualified" visitors – those more likely to purchase than to just visit your site. Also, search engines rank your Website based on the incoming links to it from respectable sites, so your page ranking is likely to go up over time too because these are all respectable sites.

How to do it:

1. Simply register on the sites below if you provide a local service or product to make it easier to be found.

Resource/s:

Local places:

www.google.com/places

http://listings.local.yahoo.com

www.bing.com/local

Share your favourite idea or success story
with other readers
On Twitter using the hash tag: **#thesalesking**
Or on the Official Facebook fanpage:
www.facebook.com/thesalesking

One contributor will be selected
to receive a free copy of
**The Sales King – Ultimate System
by Aaron Sansoni worth $4997**

IDEA 29: Write unique and valuable content for article directories and your Website

Cost: Zero if you do it yourself, or approximately $17 for a 400 word article if you use a freelance writer.

Why do it:
People love information, or at least Internet browsers love information, or specific knowledge. If you write meaningful content about your expertise, it is more likely to drive readers to your Website. Also, if the readers click on your link from a respectable article directory, the search engines consider it to be a quality link, which improves your Website page rankings.

How to do it:
1. Find a subject applicable to your niche.
2. Select the keywords you want to use in your article.
3. If you do it yourself, proceed to the next

step. If you want to hire a freelancer, use one of the resources below as a start. Simply provide your requirements as clearly as possible and then select a writer. A tip when selecting; request to see previous work so you know what your getting.

4. Upload the article either to your Website or to an article directory. If you upload the published article from an article directory onto your Website, make sure you add the whole article in its entirety, as well as the source link, otherwise you may be penalised by Google for plagiarising the article.

5. Make sure you include a resource box to get people to click on the link to take them to your Website, which is the goal of the article.

Resource/s:

Freelance writers:

www.elance.com

www.freelancewriting.com

Article directories:

www.ezine.com

www.buzzle.com

IDEA 30: Press releases

Cost: Zero if you do it yourself.

Why do it:
The objective of a press release is to demonstrate the newsworthiness of your business, product or service. The more information about your business is read, and the more awareness your business receives, the more you are likely to sell more. This is great branding for your business.

How to do it:
1. A press release has to be newsworthy and well written. If writing is not your forte, get a freelance writer to write it for you, or if you are pressed for time outsource this.

2. It's easier paying for a public relations site to syndicate your press release and it saves you a lot of time, or get a freelancer to do it for you for under $50.

Resource/s:

Free press releases:

www.pr.com

www.prlog.org

Pay annually:

www.prleap.com (pay $69 annually)

www.prweb.com (pay $89 annually)

Freelancers:

www.elance.com

IDEA 31: Email good wishes to clients on special days

Cost: Zero.

Why do it:
Most times, a special day brings back fond memories and emotions for your client. If you tap into that, it will make your client more loyal to you, and more likely to buy more from you and refer others to you. This can even be done with prospective clients. A simple 'heard it was your birthday' email can go a long way.

How to do it:
1. Simply keep a list of your clients' birthdays, wedding anniversaries, etc. and on those days, send them an email or card by post.
2. Get the information by getting them to complete a form when buying from you, or some other way including competitions for prospective clients.

Resource/s: None.

IDEA 32: Interview a local celebrity, an expert or thought leader in your niche

Cost: Zero , however buy a thank you gift for the person being interviewed for under $25.

Why do it:

People love celebrities and experts. Their opinion seems to command more respect from people. And people who are known experts in your niche will also command respect and give you credibility when associated with them. You may even be able to do a joint venture with this partner if you both can add value to each other's businesses and clients

How to do it:

1. Create a list of possible people who fit your category in your niche who you can interview, and approach them all. Think local here; well-known and respected sportsman etc. Offer something of value

to the person – consider the "what's in it for me" factor before approaching the person. Often the positive publicity is enough to attract people. Get a friend to film your interview if you can.

2. You could get the interview transcribed for $10 on Elance so you can put on your site also.

3. Well known people create hype and will bring traffic to your Website. You will also become more credible instantly.

4. Publicise it!

Resource/s:

Freelance writer to transcript:

www.elance.com

IDEA 33: Have a virtual party

Cost: Cost of the incentives/prizes.

Why do it:

Where there's fun, there's people. Also, if you give away incentives and make your virtual party fun, you can generate a lot of buzz and traffic back to your Website by making people curious enough about your business. The whole "virtual party" idea is enough of an interesting idea to get people to join in.

How to do it:

1. Get creative; celebrate a special day or anniversary of your business by having a party. Let's assume you want to create a Facebook virtual party...open your Facebook page and click on the "event" button.

2. Create your event, but before you do, plan it for maximum effect, just as if you were to have a "real" party, remembering that you are having a virtual party to

promote your Website/product/service.

3. Add incentives for people to join the party – have giveaways, specials on new products, etc.
4. Invite your Twitter followers, your Face-book friends, people who have joined your forum – everyone you can think of.

Resource/s:

Facebook:

www.facebook.com

IDEA 34: Include a service or product in a "daily deals" site

Cost: Zero. Just a 50/50 split (most of the time) with the daily deal company on the sales made from the deal.

Why do it:

If you offer a product or service of yours at a greatly reduced price, you will attract the attention of people interested in what you provide. I get an email once a week from a company who sends 3 "weekly deals" and my wife gets 4 a day! You can be sure I open it every single time, because the specials are real specials. People love getting things at greatly reduced prices. By offering your goods at a greatly reduced price, you can use this to get a flood of new people in the door in order to cross-sell and retain as clients. Remember – don't use a daily deal as a short term cash boost – they are a chance for you to create the new relationship for future business after the initial deal.

How to do it:

1. Find a Website that organises "daily deals". If necessary, find one in your area for logistical purposes.

2. You may even decide to make no profit on these customers, just so that you can get them to come in the door and keep for future purchasing.

Resource/s:

To see an example of daily deals sites:

www.groupon.com

www.scoopon.com.au

4 steps to converting a daily deal into a lifelong customer:

www.aaronsansoni.com/blog/?p=98

IDEA 35: Pop-up banners

Cost: Approximately $50 or free if you have an auto responder service.

Why do it:

Statistics show that pop-up banners in a Website, although irritating to some visitors, are likely to give you more subscribers, or take some desired action you want them to take.

How to do it:

1. If you have an auto responder service, you can do it easily through the service.
2. If you don't have an auto responder service, get a freelancer to create it for you for about $50.
3. Offer something of real value in exchange for their email address

Resource/s:

Freelance pop-up banner designer:
www.elance.com

Auto responder service:
www.aweber.com
www.getresponse.com

Share your favourite idea or success story
with other readers
On Twitter using the hash tag: **#thesalesking**
Or on the Official Facebook fanpage:
www.facebook.com/thesalesking

One contributor will be selected
to receive a free copy of
The Sales King – Ultimate System
by Aaron Sansoni worth $4997

IDEA 36: Recruit affiliate marketers

Cost: $29 one-time fee for PayDotCom (products and digital), and $49.95 one-time fee for Clickbank (digital only).

Why do it:
This idea is ideal if you have a great product but need help selling or promoting it, or if your aim is simply to increase sales.

How to do it:
1. Register with an affiliate product/digital site, like PayDotCom or Clickbank. They handle customer payments, affiliate payments, hoplinks, customer service etc.

2. I recommend that before registering; have some basic tools available for affiliates – the easier you make it for them to sell your goods, the more affiliates will sell your stuff, and the more money you'll make. These tools should include banners, ads, suggestions, a few sample email

they can use, and so on.

3. If you need help with the design, recruit a freelancer.

Resource/s:

Vendor and affiliate sites:

www.clickbank.com

www.paydotcom.com

Freelancers:

www.elance.com

IDEA 37: Network with other businesses

Cost: Zero.

Why do it:

Learn from others, and at the same time, get free exposure and links back to your Website which is great for your search engine page ranking, and of course, more visitors equals more sales.

How to do it:

1. Register for an account at a business network site. Here is where you can learn from others, and about others, generate ideas and get your business known by other members.

2. Often the best business deals are made by networking, and you get a lot of free exposure and links back to your site.

Resource/s:

Business networking:

www.betternetworker.com

IDEA 38: Hubpages

Cost: Zero.

Why do it:
Hubpages is a user generated content site. Hubpages as a site ranks high in the search engines and as a result, will get your site a lot of free exposure and will tell Google the links that are sent from Hubpages to your site are high quality.

How to do it:
1. Register at Hubpages
2. They are quite fussy, so I recommend you take the time to go through their guidelines.

Resource/s:
Hubpages:
www.hubpages.com

IDEA 39: Squidoo

Cost: Zero.

Why do it:

Squidoo is a user generated content site. It's basically a free space on the web to use as you choose. It also ranks high in the search engines and as a result, will get your site a lot of free exposure and will tell Google the links that are sent from Squidoo to your site are high quality.

How to do it:

1. Register on Squidoo and go through their guidelines and tutorials to know what you should do.

Resource/s:

Squidoo:

www.squidoo.com

IDEA 40: Submit quality articles to article submission sites

Cost: Zero.

Why do it:
Articles and links to your Website from a quality article submission site give you more credibility in the eyes of search engines, which means a higher page ranking and more traffic to your Website. This also helps with promoting your knowledge in your niche without being seen as direct or offer marketing.

How to do it:
1. Register with article submission sites and go through their guidelines. Some are quick to ban you if you don't provide high quality articles, or if you don't follow their guidelines.
2. Write articles, or if writing is not your forte, hire a freelance writer and provide

your requirements clearly.

3.   Remember to use keywords (see Idea #3).

Resource/s:

Article submission sites:

www.ezine.com

www.articledirectory.com

Share your favourite idea or success story
with other readers
On Twitter using the hash tag: **#thesalesking**
Or on the Official Facebook fanpage:
www.facebook.com/thesalesking

One contributor will be selected
to receive a free copy of
**The Sales King – Ultimate System
by Aaron Sansoni worth $4997**

IDEA 41: Add testimonials on your Website

Cost: Zero

Why do it:
Word of mouth advertising is by far the most powerful form of advertising. Testimonials from other clients tell prospective clients that you are trustworthy, honest and can deliver on your marketing promise. It's using social proof to back up your claims and is a powerful per-suader.

How to do it:
1. Get testimonials from your customers and add them to your Website in the form of written testimonials, audio or video.
2. There is nothing wrong with helping or guiding your customers to formulate what to say to best articulate their message to other prospective buyers, as long as it's their beliefs and experiences with your company.

Resource/s: None.

IDEA 42: Place free classified ads

Cost: Zero.

Why do it:

People may look for what you provide in online classifieds. I know that when I search the classifieds, I no longer search in a physical newspaper, I go online for everything I want. And so it is with many people. If you want your goods or service noticed by prospective customers, place a free ad in the classifieds. And if people link back to your site, it's more incoming links from other high ranking sites.

How to do it:

1. Register to place free classified ads. Take into account location if necessary.
2. Take the time to write your ads with your main keywords.
3. Use a logo where you can, or if you don't have a logo, use a picture as it attracts more people.

91

Resource/s:

Free classified ads:

www.adlandpro.com

www.gumtree.com

www.adpost.com

Free images:

www.sxc.hu

Share your favourite idea or success story
with other readers
On Twitter using the hash tag: **#thesalesking**
Or on the Official Facebook fanpage:
www.facebook.com/thesalesking

One contributor will be selected
to receive a free copy of
The Sales King – Ultimate System
by Aaron Sansoni worth $4997

IDEA 43: Spread a link to 17 of the best social media sites in less than 15 minutes

Cost: Zero.

Why do it:

You can choose to do it yourself, but the amount of time you'll save by using a site that automates your social media posts will give you time to do more important things to get your business promoted. If you're paying someone for SEO this might be included in the package so check with them.

How to do it:

1. Start an account with SocialMarker who will distribute a link to 17 of the best social media sites in less than 15 minutes.

Resource/s:

Spread links fast:

www.socialmarker.com

IDEA 44: Create free e-books to download from your Website

Cost: Zero if you do it yourself. $25 if you use a freelancer on Elance.

Why do it:
Online surfers love free and valuable information. If you provide a free e-book on your Website in exchange for a name and email address, more people will subscribe for it than if you were to simply ask for their details so you can send them mail! With this way, you can far more easily build a list of names you can keep in touch with so that you can build trust with them and get them to buy from you in future.

How to do it:
1. It's important to really understand your target market, because then you can target their character with an e-book they'll want to download from your Website. For instance, if your target market is driven by pleasure, teaching them about "avoid-

ing" or "mistakes" won't appeal to them, but if you create a book on "how to achieve..." you appeal to their desire for pleasure as they grow.

2. Either write the e-book yourself (it can start from 5 pages or more), or get a freelance writer to do it for you.

3. Have it published in a format that is readable on Kindle.

4. Set up your download button from your Website, again get a computer freelancer to do this.

5. Include an auto responder service if you want to get a list of people who download your e-book such as aweber.com.

Resource/s:

Publish your e-book for free:
www.lulu.com

Freelancer:
www.elance.com

Auto responder Service:
www.aweber.com

IDEA 45: Add who's recently "liked" your site

Cost: About $20 to get a programmer to add it or nothing to do it yourself.

Why do it:

If you add a Facebook Activity Feed to your Website, it gives more credibility to your Website and encourages others to participate in "liking" your site, because people like to do what other people are doing and have done. It tells them you're "good" and "safe" to do business with.

How to do it:

1. Get the Facebook Activity Feed via the link below and follow their instructions.

Resource/s:

Get the Facebook Activity Feed:

http://developers.facebook.com/docs/refer ence/plugins/activity/

Programmer to add it: www.odesk.com

IDEA 46: Get wacky, awesome and unique ideas from Fiverr – where people offer services for $5

Cost: $5.

Why do it:
This Website is just awesome! There is no other way to describe it. If you need anything done on a low budget, just browse around this Website or request it.

How to do it:
1. Go to www.fiverr.com and check out the "For $5 I will..." ideas. It will help you think out of the box.
2. Some that I saw when I checked it out for you were, "I will sing happy birthday to whoever you want and do a dance for $5" and "I will make a short animation about whatever you want for $5". How much better would it be to send a valued client

a video of a song and dance for their birthday instead of a boring old card? Or how great to use an animated character to give a message about your product? Enjoy...

Resource/s:

Fiverr:

www.fiverr.com

Share your favourite idea or success story
with other readers
On Twitter using the hash tag: **#thesalesking**
Or on the Official Facebook fanpage:
www.facebook.com/thesalesking

One contributor will be selected
to receive a free copy of
The Sales King – Ultimate System
by Aaron Sansoni worth $4997

IDEA 47: Create your own personal brand

Cost: Zero.

Why do it:

Create your own personal brand and it will help potential buyers trust you more easily – after all, people buy from people they like and trust, not from people they don't. Makes sense.

How to do it:

1. What's your brand? Let's use Sir Richard Branson as an example of creating a personal brand. Having shared the stage with Sir Richard Branson myself, I've seen first-hand how most people not only know him as the founder of the Virgin Group, but they also have a feeling of who he is as a person. This is because he has created his own personal brand. People know him to be innovative, creative, daring, caring etc. This is only because he created his own personal brand which

tells others about who he is.

2. Creating your own personal brand involves 4 steps: First take some time discover and articulate who you are as a person, then create your own brand, communicate it online via various methods, just as you would your business brand and then maintain 'Brand You'. You can even pay $97 for personal blog to be created for you and all you need to do is create posts (see resource below). Or create your own website separate from your company site promoting 'Brand You'.

Resource/s:

Personal brand sites:

www.personalbrandsites.com

Instantly Increase Your Sales in a Downward Economy – section on "Eleven ways to attack more customer right now"

www.aaronsansoni.com

IDEA 48: Exit pop-up

Cost: Zero if you already have an auto responder who provides this service.

Why do it:

This is a free way of doubling your subscribers, or getting visitors to take some type of desired action before they leave your Website.

How to do it:

1. An exit pop-up works very well, and if you offer a giveaway, doesn't make it irritating but rather can be something of real value.

2. Simply follow the instructions from your auto responder service.

3. You don't have to do it through an auto responder service for another way check out Exit Grabber.

101

Resource/s:

Auto responders:

www.mailchimp.com

www.aweber.com

www.getresponse.com

Exit banner popup software:

www.exitgrabber.com

Share your favourite idea or success story
with other readers
On Twitter using the hash tag: **#thesalesking**
Or on the Official Facebook fanpage:
www.facebook.com/thesalesking

One contributor will be selected
to receive a free copy of
**The Sales King – Ultimate System
by Aaron Sansoni worth $4997**

IDEA 49: Social proof

Cost: $20-$100 depending on what you want created and added to increase social proof

Why do it:

This is all about building trust and credibility so that you can get more people to pay for what you provide as a business.

How to do it:

1. Display recent purchases on your site. This helps encourage others to buy from you because it tells them you are credible and that others have bought from you.

2. Some ways of incorporating social proof: if you own a guesthouse, add a label to each room that says something like, "this room has been booked out 23 times this year". If you sell goods online, for one product, you could have "this item is sold out", and rotate through different items. Again, for items, you can have a label saying, "23 purchases for the past week".

3. What these labels are really saying to your visitors is, "other people have bought this, so it's safe for me to buy here too."

Resource/s:

Freelancer:

www.elance.com

Share your favourite idea or success story
with other readers
On Twitter using the hash tag: **#thesalesking**
Or on the Official Facebook fanpage:
www.facebook.com/thesalesking

One contributor will be selected
to receive a free copy of
**The Sales King – Ultimate System
by Aaron Sansoni worth $4997**

IDEA 50: RSS Feeds

Cost: Zero to set up and a few dollars to have installed by a programmer

Why do it:
Adding an RSS feed to your Website makes sure people come back and are not forever lost to you.

How to do it:
1. I'm sure you've visited a few sites which have great content, but not a lot of it. You make a mental note to return in a few weeks, but then you forget all about it. This could at times be the case for your Website too. Chances are, most people will never return. This is where an RSS feed comes in handy so that you can keep those visitors returning via your feeds.

2. Sign up at Google for a free feedburner.

Resource/s:

RSS Feedburner:

http://feedburner.google.com

Programmer:

www.elance.com

Share your favourite idea or success story
with other readers
On Twitter using the hash tag: **#thesalesking**
Or on the Official Facebook fanpage:
www.facebook.com/thesalesking

One contributor will be selected
to receive a free copy of
**The Sales King – Ultimate System
by Aaron Sansoni worth $4997**

IDEA 51: Link research

Cost: Approximately $99 a month.

Why do it:
The objective for link research is to find out who your competitors are in the online world and how much of a hill you will have to climb to surpass them.

How to do it:
1. Link research will give you the history of any domain's links in comparison to yours, analyse competitor backlinks as well as yours, compare top keywords in your niche, find opportunities in your niche – the list goes on.
2. What we can tell you for certain is that the World Wide Web revolves around links and a link research tool will certainly help give you the edge.

Resource/s:
Link research:
www.seomoz.org

* WIN *

Congratulations, as a reader of Aaron Sansoni's book you have a chance of a lifetime

Get Aaron Sansoni as your coach LIVE anywhere in the world!

That's right; Aaron will select one person each year that enters to receive the following:

- ✓ Live Full Day Meeting and Coaching Session with Aaron Sansoni for you and your business
- ✓ A copy of The Sales King Ultimate System full Home study
- ✓ Two Tickets to Aaron Sansoni live 2 day Bootcamp intensive anywhere in the world
- ✓ Personal mentoring for 6 months after your coaching with Aaron

Total Value of over $35,000!

Simply go to

www.aaronsansoni.com/win

And enter your details
It's that simple!
Terms & Conditions Apply

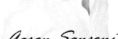

Offline Ideas

www.aaronsansoni.com

IDEA 52: Make up a seed pack

Cost: $0.50 a pack.

Why do it:
It's a memorable way to make an impact on a future customer.

How to do it:
1. Buy a small packet of cheap seeds; include a tag with your business info and a byline going something like "We're in the people growing business".
2. Keep the seed packs with you and hand out at events or use in place of the boring old business card.
3. If the seed pack is not for you think outside the box! What will give a lasting impression?

Resource/s: None.

IDEA 53: Goodie bags

Cost: $0.50 a packet.

Why do it:
People are surprised at getting little goodies for free. This idea will leave them with a good feeling, which is how you want them to relate to your business. Great idea for local business based on reoccurring relationships in the community.

How to do it:

1. Make up a bunch of small snack size zip bags with goodies in them, together with your business card or a slip of paper with your business details on it, and keep handy to give out to all you come into contact with.

2. Try to make the paper with the business details quirky, for instance...if you packed sweets into the packets, print a byline saying something like, "it's sweet doing business with us".

3. Take them into the bank with you, give one to the teller, hand out to your children's teachers, etc.

Resource/s: None.

Share your favourite idea or success story
with other readers
On Twitter using the hash tag: **#thesalesking**
Or on the Official Facebook fanpage:
www.facebook.com/thesalesking

One contributor will be selected
to receive a free copy of
**The Sales King – Ultimate System
by Aaron Sansoni worth $4997**

IDEA 54: Donate a product or service to your local radio station

Cost: Cost of the product or service you donate.

Why do it:

By donating something in exchange for publicity from a local radio station, it will work out to be far less expensive – and gives you more credibility than an ad – than having an ad created for this medium.

How to do it:

1. Offer one of your products or services to your local radio station when they next have a contest. Don't wait for them to announce a contest, but rather approach them with your offer in exchange for publicity.

2. Make sure it is something the station would like to give away and that listeners would like to try win.

Resource/s: None.

113

IDEA 55: Promote a free first consultation service

Cost: Zero.

Why do it:

The most effective way you can sell is standing in front of your prospect and engaging in full using the 7% of communication, which is your words, 38% your voice and 55% your physiology. Second to being in front of them is over the phone. If you can just get a prospective client to meet you or chat without obligation, you'll be able to really understand what they need or want, using 100% of your communication skills, and as a result you will make more sales. By offering a free first consultation, this is exactly what you're doing. If you can create trust in the free consultation, that will work out to be even better.

How to do it:

1. Offer a free consultation over the phone or face to face, or if possible, via email or

the web. Take into account that not everyone would value a face to face consultation, so offer as many ways of consulting
as possible.

2. Make sure you set a clear time and date
    where your prospect won't be distracted
    and you have enough time to build rap-
    port, understand their needs and wants
    and present a solution.

Resource/s:

The Sales King Ultimate System – DVD on "37
Ways to Strategically Increase Your Sales"

www.aaronsansoni.com

IDEA 56: Set up an employee shopping break table

Cost: The cost of your giveaways and business cards/pamphlets (around 2000 for $99).

Why do it:
Giving employees a chance to shop while at work is a novel way of getting your business known.

How to do it:
1. Approach local companies about setting up an "employee shopping break" table at lunch time where you can display your products (if the employees of the company are your target market of course), or if you provide a service, offer giveaways with your business details and free first time consultations.
2. If the company owner or managers are reluctant at first, offer them a percentage of sales made (known as 'profit-share') or maybe a free gift.

Resource/s: None.

IDEA 57: In-store promotion in a shopping mall

Cost: Cost of your giveaways.

Why do this:

Stores in shopping malls generally already get a lot of traffic. If you can set up a promotion site in the store you will save money by not paying for another venue and you are likely to make more sales and get more awareness for your business.

How to do it:

1. Do a joint venture with a store in a shopping mall. To make sure you don't have to pay fees to the shopping mall centre management, it is important that you set up your promotion in an actual store.

2. Make sure the joint venture is not with a direct competitor to you, but it must be with someone in your niche who shares your market so you can target your promotion. For example a sports retailer

could team up with a health food store as they share a similar market but don't compete.

3. You will have to consider the "what's in it for me" factor for the party you do a joint venture with, but using their store as a venue will save you on venue expenses. For example, if you sell hair products, you could approach a hair salon. In exchange for using their store as a venue, you could offer their customers a discounted price on your goodies, or a hair analysis. Be creative with approaching the other party. Make your offer irresistible, and plan your joint venture.

Resource/s:

Instantly Increase Your Sales in a Downward Economy – section on "Irresistible Offers" and "Joint Ventures"

www.aaronsansoni.com

'Tips For Lead Generation Using Outreach' video

www.Youtube.com/aaronsansonitv

IDEA 58: Donate branded tea bag wrappers to tea drinkers

Cost: $0.50 per tea bag and printed wrapper.

Why do it:
It's a good way of making people aware of your business, and it's also memorable and simple.

How to do it:
1. Create and print out tea bag wrappers with an attractive design together with your business information. Think of something clever to say on them (either a memorable quote, or something related to drinking tea and your business, like "relax with a cup of tea while we take care of you").
2. Then donate them to school teachers lounges, employee lounges, or anywhere that tea gets consumed - as long as it will get consumed by your target market of course!

Resource/s: None.

IDEA 59: Make your business official

Cost: $1 - $29.

Why do it:
If you have a great idea or a product but not yet formed a business then test your market. There are basics every business needs, and one of the things it needs is a logo and some way of telling others about what your business is about in the form of pamphlets.

How to do it:
1. You can grab a ready-made logo for $29 from www.graphicriver.net, or buy royalty free pictures from them for $1 and create your own pamphlets / business cards, etc., or buy a business card / pamphlet design for $6, saving you a lot of money on design work.
2. Then simply have the design printed. Vistaprint is a great online one-stop-shop for creating and printing marketing collateral.

Resource/s:

Ready-made logos and free images:
www.graphicriver.net
www.vistaprint.com.au

Share your favourite idea or success story
with other readers
On Twitter using the hash tag: **#thesalesking**
Or on the Official Facebook fanpage:
www.facebook.com/thesalesking

One contributor will be selected
to receive a free copy of
**The Sales King – Ultimate System
by Aaron Sansoni worth $4997**

IDEA 60: Offer a free menu design if you can add your logo

Cost: $6.

Why do it:
All the restaurant's patrons will see your logo and business details on the menu, giving you more brand awareness, and possibly more customers.

How to do it:
1. Approach local non-franchised restaurants about giving them a free menu design if you can add your logo and business details onto the menu.
2. Offer to get them printed too – at the restaurant's cost if possible.
3. Ask the restaurant for a copy of their current menu so that you can copy it's content, then go to www.graphicriver.net, select a pre-designed menu design for $6, add your logo and the menu content and get them printed.

4. Make sure before you do this, that the patrons of the restaurant are your target market.

Resource/s:

Menu designs:

www.graphicriver.net

Share your favourite idea or success story
with other readers
On Twitter using the hash tag: **#thesalesking**
Or on the Official Facebook fanpage:
www.facebook.com/thesalesking

One contributor will be selected
to receive a free copy of
**The Sales King – Ultimate System
by Aaron Sansoni worth $4997**

IDEA 61: Donate your product or service to a local charity for fundraising

Cost: Cost of the product or service.

Why do it:

Local charities are in need of donations for fundraising purposes, so if your donation to them is something worthwhile you can be sure they are going to mention it to people and market it in their fundraising, creating awareness of your business. Also, showing the community you care about charity is always a good thing and helps build trust in your business.

How to do it:

1. Approach a local charity with a proposal; as a thank you from the community, you would like to give their board members a product or service that your company provides, with the understanding that they will promote your business in any

relevant literature that they produce.

2. Make sure the charity attracts your target market, because the idea here is for the charity and its board members to promote your product for fundraising and to promote your brand to possible audiences at the same time. Board members usually network extensively, so if your donation to them is something to talk about, they likely will. The second purpose is to get your details associated with the charity because this will build trustworthiness and caring in the community where your market is.

Resource/s: None.

IDEA 62: Offer to write for your local newspaper or magazine

Cost: Zero.

Why do it:

If you're a business owner, you should be an expert in your niche, and writing for your local paper or magazine as an expert will give you excellent free publicity.

How to do it:

1. Your business information is not newsworthy to people; when you write for the paper or magazine, you need to find something about your business that is newsworthy and of interest to the community (statistics, events, etc.).

2. Make sure your article doesn't read like a long advertisement; you don't need to mention your business name until the end, or even just in your 'authors bio'

section. For newspapers and magazines to publish the article it needs to read like it belongs in their publication so a great tip here is to read and study the publication you want to get your articles featured in and copy their writing style.

Resource/s: None.

Share your favourite idea or success story with other readers
On Twitter using the hash tag: **#thesalesking**
Or on the Official Facebook fanpage:
www.facebook.com/thesalesking

One contributor will be selected
to receive a free copy of
**The Sales King – Ultimate System
by Aaron Sansoni worth $4997**

IDEA 63: Advertise in your local newspaper

Cost: Varies on readership, colour, size, etc. but generally you can place an ad for under $100.

Why do it:
Community papers do get read, especially when someone is looking for something related to their community. Actually, small businesses have found that advertising in their local newspaper instead of the big newspapers seem to bring in more clients.

Two great tips here; First, call newspaper's on their 'deadline day', which is when they need to have their ads in (just ask them for this date prior) as they have pressure to sell space. Second tip is ask them to call you if they have a 'distress' advert which means they have to fill it as there is a gap in the paper. In these instances you can buy ad space for much, much cheaper than normal.

How to do it:

1. Contact your local paper or magazine for rates and requirements.

2. Test and measure this – don't do a longer term campaign – if you don't get a response from one advert then don't do anymore or get help in writing better copy for the advert.

Resource/s:

Instantly Increase Your Sales in a Downward Economy – Section on "Writing Killer Sales Copy"

www.aaronsansoni.com

IDEA 64: Send newsletters to your customers

Cost: Depends on the method in which you send them – if you post them, it will cost more than sending them by email.

Why do it:

It's important to keep reminding your customers about your business so that when they need other services or products that are in your niche, they will come to you. Sending them newsletters helps with this.

How to do it:

1. Keep a database of your current customers and send them newsletters either monthly or bi-annually.

2. Offer good incentives in your newsletters that will encourage customers to open them including free value add items.

3. Consider your customers. Will they have access to email? Or is it better to post newsletters to them? Find out which is

more convenient for them.

4. If you email them, you can use an auto responder service to do this easily.

5. If you decide to post them, either design them, together with your content your-self, or get someone to do it for you, or get someone to create the design for you and you can add the content.

6. Get them printed and then simply post them.

Resource/s:

Auto responders:

www.mailchimp.com

www.aweber.com

www.getresponse.com

IDEA 65: Leave pamphlets at daycare centres

Cost: Varies, but you can get 2000 pamphlets for $99.

Why do it:
There are lots of parents passing through the doors of daycare centres, and as it's not the most common method of receiving a pamphlet, it's likely the pamphlet won't just be thrown away immediately. If you can get an ad in a letter to parents, do so! That's even better.

How to do it:
1. You can either choose to create the pamphlets yourself, and get them printed, which will cost you very little, or you can get a company to create them for you.
2. Or, instead of giving out pamphlets, see idea #'s 52, 53 and 58, and give those out. Generally, pamphlets can be quite effective (otherwise they would have stopped being used a long time ago!), but I think

something – any little thing – of value will be kept and remembered instead of just being tossed away. Again remember to make sure this is your market.

3. Or give a pamphlet with a difference – make it a quarter of an A4 page, staple something small on it, like a wrapped sweet, and say something relevant and catchy about it on the pamphlet.

4. Drop them off at daycare centres to be given away to parents. Perhaps give something small to the daycare owner in exchange. Always remember the "what's in it for me" factor.

Resource/s:

Instantly Increase Your Sales in a Downward Economy – Section on "Writing Killer Sales Copy"

www.aaronsansoni.com

IDEA 66: Set up a display table at events

Cost: From about $16, depending on the event. More for larger events.

Why do it:
For a very low cost (usually it is more community based), you can set up a table at events and get people aware of your business, and even make new customers, provided the event caters to your target market.

How to do it:
1. Scan local newspapers for upcoming events – look for school or church events. Or use the resource below to search for events.
2. For a small fee, set up a table where you can display your goods, or if you provide a service, have giveaways and brochures.
3. Make the table attractive.
4. Consider setting up a professionally made banner.

5. Run a competition to make it interesting and give away prizes.

Resource/s:

Search for events in your area:
www.eventbrite.com

Share your favourite idea or success story
with other readers
On Twitter using the hash tag: **#thesalesking**
Or on the Official Facebook fanpage:
www.facebook.com/thesalesking

One contributor will be selected
to receive a free copy of
**The Sales King – Ultimate System
by Aaron Sansoni worth $4997**

IDEA 67: Sponsor a goodie in New Mummy Packs at hospitals

Cost: The cost of the goodie and business information pamphlet or business card.

Why do it:

If your target market is a new parent, this is a great idea for you! There are many things new babies need, from clothing, to bedding and toys, and many parents prefer organic products, or products made by small businesses over the big commercial companies. Remember people don't worry about cost when it comes to Births, Deaths and Marriages!

How to do it:

1. Provided your target market is family related, decide what you could sponsor in New Mummy Packs at hospitals, but make sure it's something of value to a new mum.

2. Remember that new mums will not be interested in your product, unless its baby related or mum related and they see emotionally and logical benefit to their new family.

Resource/s: None.

Share your favourite idea or success story
with other readers
On Twitter using the hash tag: **#thesalesking**
Or on the Official Facebook fanpage:
www.facebook.com/thesalesking

One contributor will be selected
to receive a free copy of
**The Sales King – Ultimate System
by Aaron Sansoni worth $4997**

IDEA 68: Provide a pack of goodies to car dealerships for test drives

Cost: Under $2.50 per packet.

Why do it:
Car dealerships often have many people coming in for test drives. Giving them a small bag of goodies from your business will delight them, give your business awareness and possibly new customers, and the car dealership should be very happy to give your little packets away because they are good for their business. Remember to plan this; it's still a joint venture.

How to do it:
1. Create a mini packet of goodies with your business info and give them to car dealerships to give them to people who come in for test drives; make sure it adds value to their clients.
2. Try making what you give them relevant

to test drives or purchasing new cars and tie it in with your business. Again, you have to share a market for this like a car wash, petrol, insurance, tinting and so on.

3. Set up correctly, car dealerships should be happy to give them away, because their prospective customers will connect them to the gift as well as your company.

Resource/s: None.

IDEA 69: Get an outdoor banner

Cost: Approximately $55.

Why do it:
If you plan on taking your business to events, an outdoor banner is essential. They are inexpensive, easily viewed from a distance, and make you seem more professional and official.

How to do it:
1. Get a low cost outdoor banner printed up with your business information on it.
2. Place in a high foot traffic area. Make sure you obtain permission where necessary.

Resource/s:
Banners Online:
www.officeworks.com.au
www.vistaprint.com

IDEA 70: Run a promotional raffle with another small business store

Cost: Cost of prize or your product/service.

Why do it:

Joint ventures with the right business are always a great idea, because you save costs, each can return the favour. More heads than one provide better input to any idea. Remember to choose businesses you complement not compete with.

How to do it:

1. Join up with a local store to set up a table for a week with 3 of your best selling products, together with some pamphlets.

2. Decide on a prize and run a competition. It could either be one of your products or services, or another prize, but make sure it's of value and that the focus will be on the table with all your goodies displayed on it.

3. Collect the details of the entrants.

4. The "what's in it for me" for the store owner is the competition for his/her customers. Consider giving them a small thank-you gift and perhaps offer to have them set up a table in your store in exchange.

5. Key tip – the more you can have yourself or a staff member at the store capturing data for the raffle – the better the outcome will be – don't just leave a display and hope. Why? Because 'hope is not a strategy'.

Resource/s: None.

IDEA 71: Donate printed balloons to events

Cost: Around $55 for 2 sided printing on 200 balloons.

Why do it:

The more you get your business "out there", the more potential customers get to know about you. Printed balloons at events are professional, and for a very low amount, give your business great exposure.

How to do it:

1. Check your local paper for sporting events, or any other events. Or use the resource below.
2. Have a company supply and print on balloons, and then donate the balloons to events.
3. It would be best if you put them up yourself on the day to make sure they are not forgotten as well as maybe hand a few out along with some promotional material.

Key tip here is that if you're selling to families with children, balloons will attract the kids and by giving one out it will invite the law of reciprocity and that's your queue to chat with the parents!

Resource/s:

Search for events in your area:

www.eventbrite.com

Share your favourite idea or success story
with other readers
On Twitter using the hash tag: **#thesalesking**
Or on the Official Facebook fanpage:
www.facebook.com/thesalesking

One contributor will be selected
to receive a free copy of
The Sales King – Ultimate System
by Aaron Sansoni worth $4997

IDEA 72: Put an ad into school publications

Cost: From about $7-$40 for an ad, depending on the school and the publication.

Why do it:
Because school publications are generally looked at by many parents who want to know about their child's school days, adding an ad into a school publication is a really good idea, and it won't cost much to see if you can attack some business. Again, remember who your market is and if its parents of a school aged child or teen-ager then you're on target.

How to do it:
1. Make a list of the schools in your area, or start with the schools your kids attend.
2. Approach the schools and ask to speak with the person who arranges their events and fundraising.
3. Ask if they have any publications coming up which you can advertise in or if they

145

have any events coming up which require a program or any other documents you can advertise on. They may even produce newsletters you could advertise in.

Resource/s:

Instantly Increase Your Sales in a Downward Economy – Section on "Writing Killer Sales Copy"

www.aaronsansoni.com

Share your favourite idea or success story
with other readers
On Twitter using the hash tag: **#thesalesking**
Or on the Official Facebook fanpage:
www.facebook.com/thesalesking

One contributor will be selected
to receive a free copy of
**The Sales King – Ultimate System
by Aaron Sansoni worth $4997**

IDEA 73: Business card magnets

Cost: Around $10 for 100.

Why do it:

Business cards are good, but a business card with a difference, and one that can actually be used, is a great idea, because generally the humble little business card is simply tossed in the trash, never to be viewed by the recipient again. But one that can be used as a magnet on the fridge won't get tossed as effortlessly. Think about it, how many plumbers, electricians and food outlets are stuck on YOUR fridge!

How to do it:

1. Giving someone a business card is often a waste because more than likely it gets thrown straight into the bin. If however, you were to turn it into a magnet, it would probably be kept.

2. Find a company who makes business card magnets and then consult with them re-

147

garding the design and printing.

3. You may want to order online from the resource below.

4. Remember it's also a chance to offer more about your business than a general card and they make a great letter-box drop item.

Resource/s:

Business card magnets:

www.vistaprint.com

Share your favourite idea or success story
with other readers
On Twitter using the hash tag: **#thesalesking**
Or on the Official Facebook fanpage:
www.facebook.com/thesalesking

One contributor will be selected
to receive a free copy of
**The Sales King – Ultimate System
by Aaron Sansoni worth $4997**

IDEA 74: Throw a party for your Partner's co-workers

Cost: It can be done for under $100.

Why do it:

Trust has already been developed because of your partner's relationship with his or her co-workers. Having a party where you can display your goods just about guarantees sales and future sales if these people are your target market. Added to that, they will tell others at their workplace, and you may just get more unexpected sales through your spouses' co-workers. And why shouldn't they promote you, they love you!

How to do it:

1.   Arrange with your partner to invite their co-workers to a party.

2.   Set up a table situated in a prominent position and lay your products attractively on it.

3.   Get your guests to mingle in the area sur-

rounding the table.

4. Have a brief chat about your products, perhaps before feeding them, and then let people continue partying. Those who want more info can approach you, or collect a brochure from the table. A *soft* approach is good here – maybe start with free samples or lower priced items.

Resource/s: Your Partner! ☺

IDEA 75: Put a pamphlet on your local store bulletin board

Cost: The cost of the pamphlet!

Why do it:

It costs next to nothing, and as you frequent the local store anyway, you lose nothing. And believe it or not, those bulletin boards are actually read, and again, you are creating awareness in the community about your business. Don't just look for the one idea to move mountains, the more of these ideas you try the better your chances of taking your business to the next level

How to do it:

1. After receiving permission from the store manager, put a pamphlet on the local store bulletin board, or even better, get the store manager to agree that you can speak to customers upon their exit.

2. Consider offering something of value to customers. Think big value not just a straight sale or discount. Why not try giving them something for free?

151

Resource/s:

Instantly Increase Your Sales in a Downward Economy – Section on "Writing Killer Sales Copy"

www.aaronsansoni.com

Share your favourite idea or success story
with other readers
On Twitter using the hash tag: **#thesalesking**
Or on the Official Facebook fanpage:
www.facebook.com/thesalesking

One contributor will be selected
to receive a free copy of
**The Sales King – Ultimate System
by Aaron Sansoni worth $4997**

IDEA 76: Offer easy shopping for senior citizens

Cost: Zero.

Why do it:

Provided they are your target market, taking your products to a senior citizen housing facility will be appreciated as it is sometimes difficult for seniors to get to shops, and you will make sales if you make it easy for them to buy from you.

How to do it:

1. Offer easy shopping for Senior Citizens at Senior housing facilities. Note that we don't mean old aged homes, but rather complexes where senior citizens have bought property to live out their retirement.

2. If you're going to go face to face for this, I hope you like good long chats and cups of tea!

Resource/s: None.

IDEA 77: Leave pamphlets on car windshields

Cost: $6 – grab a pamphlet design from Graphic River and printing is about $65 for 2500.

Why do it:
Again, it's all about awareness and getting your business visible in the community. And in the process, you may just make an extra client or two.

How to do it:
1. Get permission from your local shopping centre management to leave pamphlets or postcards on car windshields.
2. You can grab a pamphlet design from Graphic River, or order from your local printing store.

Resource/s:

Ready-made pamphlet designs:

www.graphicriver.net

www.aaronsansoni.com

Instantly Increase Your Sales in a Downward Economy – Section on "Writing Killer Sales Copy" & "Irresistible Offers"

IDEA 78: Hold workshops

Cost: It can be done for under $100.

Why do it:
This is a great way to show your expertise. You can either charge a small fee (just so that they appreciate the workshop more), or none at all. They will be grateful to you and this will result in word of mouth advertising. Maximise the benefit by asking them to give a testimonial, participate in your social media campaigns and/or complete a survey.

How to do it:
1. As an expert in your niche, offer to teach classes to adults at churches, high schools, colleges and community centres.
2. For instance, if you sell candles, offer a class on how to decorate them. If you sell a weight loss product, offer an accountability class. If you provide a business strategy service, hold a workshop on how to start your own small business.

3. Charge a low fee, and keep a database of attendants so that you can up sell them when the time is right as well as offer on-going value.

4. Make the most of the experience and advertise the event on Facebook, Twitter, etc. Take photos and put them on Facebook and tag people so that their friends see them too.

Resource/s:

Event registration, marketing and payment service:

www.eventbrite.com

IDEA 79: Create paper gifts

Cost: Approximately $0.10 per gift.

Why do it:
People like getting things they can use, and if something is attractive, well that's even better. And it's always visible to them, so when they need something you provide, they are likely to call you if you continually remind them about your business!

How to do it:
1. Create "paper gifts" - bookmarks, gift tags, shopping lists, etc. with your business details, and hand these out wherever you go.
2. Probably a better idea than the business card; you just need to get creative.
3. If you are creative, you could make them yourself, or have them printed.

Resource/s:
   www.vistaprint.com

IDEA 80: Make your own re-ordering contact details for your products

Cost: Approximately $0.20 for 10 labels.

Why do it:
It's a lot cheaper to do it yourself, and making it easy for your customers to order again by having your details close at hand makes good business sense.

How to do it:
1. Make it easy for your customers to order again by creating and printing out your own re-ordering labels for your products. Alternatively you can create this online with customer login and reordering functions or even automatic reordering to keep up the supply they need.
2. For actual labels, make them easy to see.
3. Think carefully about the durability of the label. For instance, you may need a label

for a shampoo bottle that can withstand water. Otherwise, create a fridge magnet with a catchy slogan to remind them where to call to replace their shampoo.

Resource/s:

www.vistaprint.com

Share your favourite idea or success story
with other readers
On Twitter using the hash tag: **#thesalesking**
Or on the Official Facebook fanpage:
www.facebook.com/thesalesking

One contributor will be selected
to receive a free copy of
**The Sales King – Ultimate System
by Aaron Sansoni worth $4997**

IDEA 81: Get a free business card design

Cost: Zero for the design, just pay for the printing (around $36 for 250).

Why do it:

You can probably save a whole lot on the design work by doing it this way, and your cards will still look professional.

How to do it:

1. Get a free business card design from www.vistaprint.com and then get the business cards printed locally or occasionally companies like Vista will print them for free if you pay the postage. It's a good starter when you're not looking to spend a lot in the early stages of your business.

Resource/s:

Free business card designs:

www.vistaprint.com

IDEA 82: Referral coupons

Cost: Around $99 for 2000.

Why do it:
People like saving and getting things for free, that's why these are usually so successful! Giving your customers an incentive to bring you more customers just makes sense, and they are likely to try and help you this way if they get something in return.

How to do it:
1. Create referral coupons and offer regular customers a free little gift or personal discount if they refer a new customer to you.
2. Attach it to a newsletter or to a product that is bought, or if you offer a service, attach it to the invoice.

Resource/s:
www.vistaprint.com

IDEA 83: Create kids colouring pages

Cost: Zero.

Why do it:

Where do the pictures kids draw or colour in end up? On fridges! Fridges are probably the most looked at piece of furniture in the house, so it's a great idea advertising on kids colouring pages! Great idea if your target market is kids or families.

How to do it:

1. Have some kids colouring pages printed (or grab some free ones from the resource below).

2. In a small space, copy your logo onto it, together with a "Courtesy of (your business name)".

3. Give them away to local restaurants and nursery schools and any other business where kids are brought along and there's space for children's activities.

Resource/s:

Download free kids colouring pages:
www.colouring-pages-kids.com

Share your favourite idea or success story
with other readers
On Twitter using the hash tag: **#thesalesking**
Or on the Official Facebook fanpage:
www.facebook.com/thesalesking

One contributor will be selected
to receive a free copy of
**The Sales King – Ultimate System
by Aaron Sansoni worth $4997**

IDEA 84: Make your car a moving advertisement

Cost: Around $55.

Why do it:
Provided your car is in good shape, advertising on it will give you a lot of exposure. I know I have contacted at least 2 companies very recently whose ads were on their cars. And it's relatively cheap. Also if you can convince them, having the advertisement on family member's cars helps your exposure.

How to do it:
1. Choose what you want featured on the magnet; generally it will be your logo with your contact details featured prominently.

2. Many online companies that produce car magnets will also help with the design. Vistaprint is a great example of a company that does this.

3. Consider size and number of magnets; do

you want one on each side of your car? If you have a bigger car then you should opt for a bigger size for maximum visibility.

Resource/s:

www.vistaprint.com

www.aaronsansoni.com

Instantly Increase Your Sales in a Downward Economy – Section on "Writing Killer Sales Copy"

IDEA 85: Re-admission hand stamp advertising

Cost: About $50.

Why do it:
Brand awareness. Pure and simple. And it's cheap. And different.

How to do it:
1. First approach clubs or events and offer to sponsor the re-admission hand stamps if you can put your logo on the stamp. Check for events at the resource below.
2. Find a company who makes the stamps and find out if they can add your logo to the stamp.

Resource/s:
Companies who can create hand stamps:
www.speedystamps.co.uk
www.vistaprint.com
or your local office supplies company

Check for events in your area:
www.eventbrite.com

IDEA 86: Leave flyers in gym lockers

Cost: About $99 for 2000 flyers.

Why do it:

People who use gym lockers are almost certain to carry bags. If your pamphlet is in the gym locker, they will either look at it (because it carries more weight coming from their gym), or place it in their bag to look at it later. Again, it's about brand awareness and getting your business visible to the public. Could your target market be health conscious people?

How to do it:

1. Approach your local gym about leaving flyers in the changing room lockers. Offer them something in return; it can't just be about your benefit.

2. Make sure it's in an prominent area and think about the target market when writing the advert

Resource/s:

www.vistaprint.com

www.aaronsansoni.com

Instantly Increase Your Sales in a Downward
Economy Homestudy

The Sales King Ultimate System Homestudy

Share your favourite idea or success story
with other readers
On Twitter using the hash tag: **#thesalesking**
Or on the Official Facebook fanpage:
www.facebook.com/thesalesking

One contributor will be selected
to receive a free copy of
**The Sales King – Ultimate System
by Aaron Sansoni worth $4997**

IDEA 87: Donate a product for a newspaper contest

Cost: Cost of the product.

Why do it:
Great publicity that is worth more than plain advertising. PT Barnum, a founder of publicity, said "A terrible thing happens without publicity ... NOTHING!"

How to do it:
1. Donate one of your products or services for a local area newspaper or a magazine with your target market. Allow them to use this in a contest. Remember it needs to be of huge value or they will charge you like an advertisement. Start small with this and approach smaller publications that are read by your market.

Resource/s:
www.Youtube.com/aaronsansonitv
- 'Getting Free Publicity' video

IDEA 88: Direct mailing to your target market

Cost: Approximately $80 for 50,000 names.

Why do it:

I would never recommend you buying a direct mailing list that contains random names of people who are not in your target market. But using a list that contains names of people who have indicated some type of interest in your niche just may get you a few sales, considering you would be sending to so many people. If you can afford to spend more, you can buy a keyword targeted list for approximately $249 for 50,000 names.

How to do it:

1. Direct mailing companies can break down a database into categories of ages, genders, areas, lifestyles, hobbies etc.
2. If you know your target market then buying a targeted list is a good idea.
3. Find a company that specialises in direct

mailing lists – I would suggest going online to do initial research.

4. Find comments that have been made about the success rate of lists from a particular company if you can.

Resource/s:

www.Youtube.com/aaronsansonitv

- 'Guide to Marketing using Direct Mail' video

IDEA 89: Speak as an expert and promote your business

Cost: Zero.

Why do it:

If you're a confident speaker, offer to speak as an expert at a relevant event. This is a really good idea, because it costs you nothing except your time, and because you are speaking as an expert, you already get an edge on the trust factor. Speak in exchange for free publicity or if you can mention your business in your speech.

How to do it:

1. Network with other businesses so you can get news of upcoming events in your niche, or scan newspapers and online for event ads.
2. Offer to speak as an expert in exchange for publicity.

Resource/s:

Search for events in your area or hold one yourself:

www.eventbrite.com

IDEA 90: Organise a free information evening

Cost: Cost of venue and light beverages – can be done for under $100.

Why do it:
This has been a very popular way to get new business. If guests feel they will benefit from the evening, they will attend and you will have a chance to speak about what you do, making sales and creating awareness.

How to do it:
1. Think of what prospective clients would like to know about in your niche, and then organise a free information evening where you provide the answers.
2. Keep it relatively short, and don't just advertise your business at this medium, but rather focus on providing value, with a snippet of your business information.
3. An example: you sell weight loss products. Your free information evening could

be on cooking tips for weight loss. Have a demonstration and let everyone have tasters.

4. At the same time, have a table with your products on display, and keep them on hand so people can buy immediately. Consider using your office or home as a venue so that you can save costs.

5. Hand out pamphlets and promote to your database.

Resource/s:

List your event for free:

www.eventbrite.com

IDEA 91: Do follow-up calls

Cost: Cost of the telephone call.

Why do it:
You can find out a lot about your offering, your staff, and have a second chance at selling.

How to do it:
1. Call all prospective clients who don't go ahead with your product or service the week after they have spoken with someone in your office.
2. This "double up" method should be a courtesy call/survey to see how the prospect found your service.
3. Use the opportunity to strategise and structure your questions so that you find out a lot about your offering and your staff.
4. Include a way of getting a 2nd opportunity to sell.
5. Consider making this part of your sales process.

Resource/s:

The Sales King Ultimate System – DVD on "37 Ways to Strategically Increase Your Sales"
www.aaronsansoni.com

Share your favourite idea or success story
with other readers
On Twitter using the hash tag: **#thesalesking**
Or on the Official Facebook fanpage:
www.facebook.com/thesalesking

One contributor will be selected
to receive a free copy of
The Sales King – Ultimate System
by Aaron Sansoni worth $4997

IDEA 92: Give away free coffee cards to the local café in exchange for filling out a survey

Cost: Cost of the coffee and a coffee card.

Why do it:

People will help you provided you make it worth their while. By offering them something small in exchange for their time to complete a targeted survey, they will take the time to provide the information you require, which will help you know your target market better, and give you a better understanding of how to market your business. It's also a good way of not directly selling but capturing data and doing 'Needs Analysis' at the same time.

How to do it:

1. The survey should ask specific questions about the needs and wants of your prospective customer regarding your product

or service.

2. Make sure the questions are targeted.

3. You can use the coffee concept or replace with a free 5 - 10 minute massage at the local massage shop. Use something that would be of value to them and that they will give their time for.

4. Arrange with the local café or massage shop.

5. Think of ways of approaching people who are interested in your niche.

Resource/s:

The Sales King Ultimate System – Sections on "The Sales Process"

www.aaronsansoni.com

IDEA 93: Give waiting parents something to do

Cost: Cost of pamphlets and sample.

Why do it:

Parents wait in their cars for their children to come out of school. This is an opportune time for them to read a pamphlet together with a free sample, giving your business more awareness if this is your target market.

How to do it:

1. Go to schools in your area and at the time the school finishes.

2. Give parents waiting in their cars a pamphlet, and where possible, a sample of something that would be appreciated.

3. If possible, make the pamphlet applicable to "waiting for kids" so that it's memorable.

4. Get their details in exchange for a sample or free goodie.

Resource/s:

www.vistaprint.com

www.aaronsansoni.com

Instantly Increase Your Sales in a Downward Economy – Section on "Writing Killer Sales Copy"

Share your favourite idea or success story
with other readers
On Twitter using the hash tag: **#thesalesking**
Or on the Official Facebook fanpage:
www.facebook.com/thesalesking

One contributor will be selected
to receive a free copy of
The Sales King – Ultimate System
by Aaron Sansoni worth $4997

IDEA 94: Use a loss leader to data capture prospective clients

Cost: Zero but the cost price of your product or service.

Why do it:
Giving one of your small, low cost products away or selling it at cost price for a limited time in order to capture prospective clients is a good idea to capture clients you can create a relationship with and up sell to. Think of big supermarkets and retailers who use catalogues with "specials". The front page is usually loss leaders to draw you into reading further and going into the store.

They know that once you are in the door, you will spend money on other products and not only the sale goods. The sale goods merely act as a "hook" to bring you through their doors.

How to do it:

1. Copying this tried and tested formula, you can attract the same results.
2. Find a product of greatest appeal and lowest cost price for you to produce
3. Market this at the cost price or as free ensuring you capture all details on the transaction for future sales marketing.

Resource/s: None.

IDEA 95: Offer a free service together with your main service or product

Cost: Depends on what you decide to offer.

Why do it:
It's important to make it easy for customers to do business with you. If you offer a free service together with your main service or product, you're adding perceived value and will attract a lot more customers, and keep them.

How to do it:
Let's use a hair salon as an example...

1. Put yourself in your customer's shoes: your client has brought her 3 year old child with her, but the child gets bored and keeps bugging her while her hair is being done. Do you think this is a good experience for your client? No it's not. She would probably prefer not to come to the hair salon with her child in future.

2. Now make it easy for her – give her a good experience and she will return to your hair salon.

3. Simply put a kid's table and chair in the salon, so that the child can draw and colour in. Add a few toys, and both mum and child are happy.

4. Think of how you can make it easy for your customers to do business with you and how you can add massive perceived value compared to the actual cost you're asking.

Resource/s: None.

IDEA 96: Offer your staff incentives to promote the business

Cost: Cost of the incentive.

Why do it:
If your staff can benefit by bringing in new customers, they are going to be motivated to do so. Use the opportunity to get your staff to promote your business to their friends and family, and in the process, increase their loyalty to you!

How to do it:
1. Think of ways you can create incentives for new business your staff bring. Even better, get them to tell you what they would like in exchange for bringing in new business.
2. Make it a set standard, so it's clear what they will get in return for selling items / services of different values. Every person

in your business is a walking talking advertisement, it's up to you to engage them in the process

Resource/s:

The Sales King Ultimate System – DVD on "37 Ways to Strategically Increase Your Sales"

www.aaronsansoni.com

IDEA 97: Organise a community day

Cost: If done properly, it won't need to cost you anything.

Why do it:
You receive great, free publicity that you could not achieve by just placing an ad in your local newspaper.

How to do it:
1. First approach your local charity about items they need (for babies, it could be nappies, cream, bibs, etc., or for animals it could be blankets, tin food etc.).
2. Then approach your local newspaper about your community day – people bring in 3 needed items for the charity and they will get a huge discount on their purchases. You may find that the local newspaper will be happy to advertise your community day for free.
3. Arrange for your newspaper to show a

picture of the collection at the end of the period, or the hand-over of goods to the charity.

Resource/s:

www.aaronsansoni.com

Instantly Increase Your Sales in a Downward Economy – Section on "Joint Ventures"

Share your favourite idea or success story
with other readers
On Twitter using the hash tag: **#thesalesking**
Or on the Official Facebook fanpage:
www.facebook.com/thesalesking

One contributor will be selected
to receive a free copy of
The Sales King – Ultimate System
by Aaron Sansoni worth $4997

IDEA 98: Get people to sell to their friends and family for commission

Cost: The commission on products that are sold.

Why do it:
There may be other people who are great at selling things to their family and friends. If they can sell your goods, offer them commission. They don't have to be employees of your company, just people who get others to buy from you.

How to do it:
1. Get people on board to sell for you, and give them commission when they make a sale. You may find they will do it for nothing if you get them engaged into your business and vision.
2. Give them terms so they know what the guidelines are, and provide the tools they need to make sales, even if you need to do it for a fee.

Resource/s:

The Sales King Ultimate System Homestudy
www.aaronsansoni.com

Share your favourite idea or success story
with other readers
On Twitter using the hash tag: **#thesalesking**
Or on the Official Facebook fanpage:
www.facebook.com/thesalesking

One contributor will be selected
to receive a free copy of
The Sales King – Ultimate System
by Aaron Sansoni worth $4997

IDEA 99: Join your local Chamber of Commerce

Cost: Varies by country.

Why do it:
This can be a great way to get your business out in the community for very little cash outlay. They offer programs and services free for their members, and often refer business to their members.

How to do it:
1. Simply find your local Chamber of Commerce – it would be fastest to look for them online. Search by area.
2. See what they offer.
3. Join!

Resource/s: None.

IDEA 100: Human sign

Cost: Under $30 for one sign plus payment to "human sign" for about $20.

Why do it:

Business exposure at a very low cost. You don't have to pay for space because the sign is not stationary.

How to do it:

1. Have an attractive sign made that a human can "wear" comfortably.
2. Hire someone (or use a volunteer!) to "wear" it in a high traffic area for the day, and where your target market frequents.
3. If it's not stationary, you may get away with your "human sign" handing out pamphlets too.
4. Make sure the person you use is not shy, and have some fun with this!

Resource/s:

Instantly Increase Your Sales in a Downward Economy – Section on "Writing Killer Sales Copy"

www.aaronsansoni.com

Share your favourite idea or success story
with other readers
On Twitter using the hash tag: **#thesalesking**
Or on the Official Facebook fanpage:
www.facebook.com/thesalesking

One contributor will be selected
to receive a free copy of
The Sales King – Ultimate System
by Aaron Sansoni worth $4997

IDEA 101: Sponsor a school's concert programme and add your logo

Cost: Under $40 for the design and printing of the programme (quantity of 250).

Why do it:

A school's concert programme gets viewed and is not thrown straight in the trash, with many parents even keeping it for sentimental reasons. You can get a lot of exposure for a very small cost.

How to do it:
1. Approach schools in your area about concerts, especially at the end of the year, but approach them well in advance and offer to sponsor the concert programmes on condition that you can add your logo and business details.
2. Consider adding a coupon to the programme, but don't make them have to cut the programme to redeem it.

Resource/s: None.

Resources – Alphabetised

Affiliate and vendor sites:
www.clickbank.com
www.paydotcom.com

Article directories:
www.ezine.com
www.buzzle.com

Article submission sites:
www.ezine.com
www.articledirectory.com

Auto Responders:
www.mailchimp.com
www.aweber.com
www.getresponse.com

Banners Online:
www.officeworks.com.au
www.vistaprint.com

"Best of" Ideas:
www.listofbests.com

Business card magnets:
www.vistaprint.com

Business networking:

www.betternetworker.com

Classified ads - free:

www.adlandpro.com

www.adpost.com

www.gumtree.com

Colouring pages – free downloads:

www.colouring-pages-kids.com

Coupon code software - free:

www.imsoftxtreme.com/coupon-codes

Daily deals sites:

www.groupon.com

www.scoopon.com.au

Domain name availability:

www.namecheap.com

E-commerce sites:

www.etsy.com

www.ebay.com

Events search:

www.eventbrite.com

Exit banner popup software:

www.exitgrabber.com

Facebook Activity Feed:
http://developers.facebook.com/docs/referen
ce/plugins/activity/

Fiverr:
www.fiverr.com

Freelance pop-up banner designer:
www.elance.com

Freelance writers:
www.elance.com
www.freelancewriting.com

Google Adwords:
www.google.com/ads/adwords

Guest writing site to get you started:
www.guestblogit.com

Hosts:
www.bluehost.com
www.godaddy.com
www.hostgator.com

Hubpages:
www.hubpages.com

**Instantly Increase Your Sales In A Downward
Economy Homestudy:**
www.aaronsansoni.com/store.php

Images - free:

www.sxc.hu

Keyword Research:

www.googlekeywordtool.com

Link research:

www.seomoz.org

Local places:

www.google.com/places

http://listings.local.yahoo.com

www.bing.com/local

Logos (ready made) and images:

www.graphicriver.net

Menu designs:

www.graphicriver.net

News sites:

www.topsy.com

www.wesmirch.com

www.popURLs.com

Online freelance content writers:

www.elance.com

www.freelancewriting.com

Online tools:

www.googlekeywordtool.com

www.google.com/reader
www.google.com/analytics

Online video features:
www.viddler.com

Personal brand sites:
www.personalbrandsites.com

Press release help - pay annually:
www.prleap.com (pay $69 annually)
www.prweb.com (pay $89 annually)

Press releases - free:
www.pr.com,
www.prlog.org

Programmer:
www.odesk.com
www.elance.com

Publish your e-book for free:
www.lulu.com

Q&A Forum:
www.answers.yahoo.com
http://uk.answers.yahoo.com
www.question.com

RSS Feedburner:
http://feedburner.google.com

SEO Company:
www.attracta.com

Social networks – update all at once:
https://seesmic.com
www.socialmarker.com

Squidoo:
www.squidoo.com

Stamps – re-admission hand stamps:
www.speedystamps.co.uk

Text link ads companies:
www.textlinkads.com
www.textlinkbrokers.com

Traffic exchange:
www.trafficswarm.com

The Sales King Ultimate System:
www.aaronsansoni.com/store.php

Viral marketing campaign example:
www.willitblend.com

Vendor and affiliate sites:
www.clickbank.com
www.paydotcom.com

Videos – browse or upload:

www.youtube.com

Web directories – respectable and affordable:

www.dmoz.org

www.goguides.org

Website builders - free:

www.weebly.com

www.wix.com

* WIN *

Congratulations, as a reader of Aaron Sansoni's book you have a chance of a lifetime

Get Aaron Sansoni as your coach LIVE anywhere in the world!

That's right; Aaron will select one person each year that enters to receive the following:

✓ Live Full Day Meeting and Coaching Session with Aaron Sansoni for you and your business
✓ A copy of The Sales King Ultimate System full Home study
✓ Two Tickets to Aaron Sansoni live 2 day Bootcamp intensive anywhere in the world
✓ Personal mentoring for 6 months after your coaching with Aaron

<u>Total Value of over $35,000!</u>

Simply go to
www.aaronsansoni.com/win
And enter your details
It's that simple!
Terms & Conditions Apply

Aaron Sansoni

9 781481 026208